TIME
WITHOUT
YOU

BY MARY BRADY

First published in 2009 by

MESSENGER
PUBLICATIONS
JESUITS in IRELAND

Messenger Publications, 37 Lower Leeson Street, Dublin 2
www.messenger.ie

Printed in Ireland

ISBN 978-1-872245-74-4

Typeset in 10/18 Times Regular

COVER IMAGE:
DERMOT
43CM X 43CM
EMBROIDERY ON HANDKERCHIEF
BY MARY BRADY

Dedicated to

DERMOT

February 23rd, 1925 ~ October 24th, 2001

This is a personal work of grief. It includes some of my paintings, drawings, poems, embroideries and diary entries. Some I did before my husband died and some were made after his death.

Dermot writing

Mary Brady 1990

PENCIL ON PAPER

OPERATIONS
92CM X 61CM
OIL & MIXED MEDIA ON CANVAS

DIARY ENTRIES

3rd August, 2000

Dermot is not feeling great today. He says his heart feels heavy at night and his energy is very poor. I'm scared a lot of the time. Anticipating what lies ahead or what I imagine lies ahead. How can I know what lies ahead? Yet I have to try and prepare myself otherwise when I look at it, it seems a big muddle of pain and anxiety and out of control. And I generally turn away from it in my thoughts. I don't want to face a future like that, a future without him.

8th August, 2000

Dermot is resting on the sofa in his workroom. He feels exhausted he says though he is not long up. The day is warm. It is hard going and he is going down hill slowly. Sometimes I see it clearly and my heart feels as if it had been squeezed tight, it's so painful. I am terrified at what might lie ahead of us. He is so frail and he feels his heart hurts though he takes three injections a week now.

September 11th, 2000

Dermot is not well at all. The least effort exhausts him. When he feels like this I usually need to take him to the Hospital. I hate him being on a trolley all day waiting for a bed, when he feels so wretched. Someday he won't come home. It breaks my heart.

January 26th, 2001

Dermot got a blockage in his kidney on the Thursday before Christmas. I had to take him to the Hospital. His blood pressure dropped and he was sick and in pain. I thought all hopes for a Christmas at home were gone. Last year he had pneumonia and was there over the Millennium New Year. But this year, thank God, he came home on Christmas Eve, shaky and feeble and not hungry but at least home. I'm scared it will be our last together.

ANGUISH
41CM X 30CM
INK & CHARCOAL & CRAYON

KIDNEYS

TIME WITHOUT YOU

My husband died in October 2001 after an illness of more than ten years. It began with a Hepatitis C infection from a blood transfusion and ended in kidney cancer. When cancer was first diagnosed he was given a year to live. We both found this very hard to accept and we looked around for ways that we might be able to extend his life. There was plenty on offer in diets and treatments so I changed his diet and he changed his lifestyle and began meditation. I prayed for his recovery as I'd never prayed before. At the end of the year he was no worse and had even put on some weight. But his cancer was a relentless enemy and not easily defeated. We did slow down its progress and he got six extra years but it seemed we were fighting a losing battle.

To begin with I found it hard to believe he would die even though I was aware of his deterioration. It just seemed impossible, unreal. When I could no longer deny the reality of what was happening and his stays in hospital became more frequent I began to draw and paint my reaction to his suffering, my anger, my confusion, my fear and my sadness. In some Art I bargained with God, in some I struggled with my fear of what lay ahead, in some I put feelings for which I could not find words. I also made kidneys in different materials: clay, plaster and fabric. Some were bleeding and sore which I bandaged and stitched, some were hard like stone, some soft and jewelled. I made glass containers to hold them. Bit by bit as I made them my feelings of anger began to drain away and I began to see that I had to accept the diseased kidneys, as I had to accept Dermot's deteriorating health if I was going to be able to accompany him on his journey towards death, with the support he needed. Giving physical shape to and making concrete, the muddle of conflicting feelings inside me, helped me cope with them. Giving them a presence made them more understandable. The work I did became the symbols that held the pain I felt. I thought of them as physical prayers, votive offerings. They helped keep me steady through those years.

Watching this man I loved suffer, day after day, and gradually lose his ability to do the things he enjoyed and eventually the ability to do things for himself, was heartbreaking. So even though I felt I had begun the grieving process before he died, nothing prepared me for the reality. I knew death for him was a relief from pain but I found the irrevocability of it a terrible shock. "Love

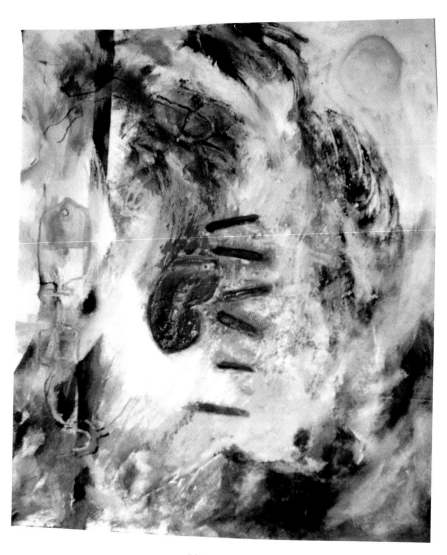

HOSPITAL
41CM X 30CM
OIL & MIXED MEDIA ON PAPER

HOSPITAL
77cm x 92cm
OIL & MIXED MEDIA ON CANVAS

knows not its depth until the hour of separation." When he died it was just as if I had had no preparation at all. I simply couldn't believe it had happened, that he was gone forever and that I would never again see or hear or talk to the man that I had loved and lived with for most of my life.

Recovery from the loss of a loved one is a long and difficult process. There is no easy way to deal with it. It seems we have to go through the rooms of grief as best we can, through the shock and denial, the longing and searching, the anger and guilt, the despair and unutterable sadness, until we come to some measure of acceptance.

The initial numbness that followed his death was a sort of protection from the awful realisation of what had happened. For weeks everything was unreal, I forgot things, I confused things, and I couldn't make the simplest decision. Going to sleep was difficult and I didn't feel like eating, and I couldn't pray. My body was sore. It felt as if I had lost a layer of skin. I felt lost and adrift in a black fog. And the journey out of this awful overwhelming grief was like recovering from a serious illness.

There were things that helped me cope. Having people around who cared about me and were willing to listen and let me cry without stopping helped a lot. I cried until I was exhausted and I howled loudly when I was alone in the house or sometimes driving the car. I found this a great release. I was fortunate in having a loving family member to look after me in the early weeks and a friend who was widowed and understood how I was feeling.

Meditation was also a help, calming my body and mind and creating a space inside me that wasn't filled with pain.

In the early months everywhere I went, everything I saw or heard, stirred memories that set me back in a dark place of loss: music on the radio, a car that looked like his, seeing his name on letters that continued to come for him, or places we had walked together. And everyday I woke to a feeling of anguish before I remembered why. Life had lost its meaning. All the things I took for granted were gone. It was like the turn of a kaleidoscope when the configuration changes. Everything seemed the same but actually everything had changed forever. My beliefs, my certainties, my identity even were in question. I had no answers to anything. It was like drifting in the dark on the open sea.

Then six months later a friend told me about a group called Bethany who supports those who are grieving. I arrived at the Bethany meeting feeling that I was bleeding to death from a deep wound that would never heal. But here I found I was not alone. One of the things that it is possible to do with the terrible pain of loss is to share it and share the things that help us survive. Other people's coping strategies can help us. Listening to people sharing their grief, I was reassured to learn that others had also experienced what I was going through. I was reassured that it was alright to feel despair and anguish, to feel anger and fear and confusion. No, I was not abnormal or going mad and yes, one day I would feel better. The meetings lessened my feelings of loneliness and isolation.

Initially a Bethany member came to my house once a week. She listened to my endless repetitions of loss and grief. We shared a love of books and she brought me things to read that she thought would help, articles and poems written by people whose loved ones had died. They had gone through what I was going through and had survived it and this held out some hope for me. Their journeys were similar to mine. She supported all my efforts to take steps to heal the wound, to visit and go places with friends, to help focus my attention outside myself and allow the pain to subside.

After Dermot's death, I didn't feel the same need to give a visual shape to my feelings as I had during his illness, but I continued to keep a diary. I began to write poems, which I had never done before. I also felt a need to collect or contain Dermot's life in some way; to give it meaning and shape, to make something tangible that would hold his story and recognise his uniqueness. So I began to compile a book of his life. Because the dead have no voice of their own and it is easy to distort their views, I used his diaries as a basis. A book would be something I could leave behind me for our children and grandchildren. I had to learn a computer programme to enable me to achieve this, using photographs, drawings, cards, cuttings and extracts from his diaries. I included all the memorabilia collected over years by his mother, old school reports and certificates, badges and medals, and even an old tram ticket for 2d. It was the fare to his childhood home in Monkstown. I wrote down all I could remember of the stories he had told me about his family and childhood. Then I printed out four copies, made covers for them and had them bound. It took me almost two years to complete it, but in making it I felt I had relived his life with him and it was very therapeutic for me.

I discovered that it is less the content of these works, whether they are made with paint or clay or words, but more the way we do them, that counts. It was the fact that I had made them; that I had given shape and physicality to my feelings, that allowed me to access my grief and helped

BARGAINING
91CM X 76CM
OIL & MIXED MEDIA ON CANVAS

FEAR
76CM X 91 CM
OIL & MIXED MEDIA ON CANVAS

my work of mourning. Art in whatever forms it takes, often links creation with loss.

Two-and-a-half years after my husband died I decided to walk some of the Camino de Santiago de Compostela. I needed to collect myself, to do something that would help me know myself as a person who could survive alone, could make decisions and could begin a life that was meaningful in a different way. My Bethany supporter and friend encouraged me to go. She drove me to the airport bus and we sang the hymn "To Be a Pilgrim" to keep up my spirits on the way. Three weeks later, when I limped into the Plaza Obradoire in Santiago, which was filled with pilgrims, I knew I would never be quite the same. In the great Cathedral I was surrounded by pilgrims from all over the world; perhaps many of them there because of loss in their lives. I was awe-struck by the huge censor, the *Botafumeiro*, swinging over our heads as it had been doing since the Middle Ages. During the pilgrimage Mass I began to understand the brotherhood of suffering, the incredible gift life is and how precious is every moment of our lives. Suffering is not a way I would choose to learn, but there are some things that only suffering can teach. Now my heart knows.

Do I conduct this symphony
That is my life?
Or does another wield the bato
One who chose the theme
Who writes the music
In B flat Minor?
And am I just the musician
Following the score?

DIARY ENTRIES

7th November, 2001

Dermot's funeral was this day two weeks ago. I still don't believe he has gone. Dermot has gone forever. He will never be back. I will never talk to him again, or hug him or hear his voice again. I do not believe it. But finding his wallet with his cards and a five euro note stuck in it, in his anorak pocket was a shock, as if I had been stabbed in my chest. He was using it such a very short time ago, going down to the village for the paper with his stick. Very frail it's true but still there and enjoying things. I can't believe we won't be together again.

10th November, 2001

I drift from day to day, hoping the pain and fear will go, numb and unable to think of anything. The pain of loss is terrible. I yearn for Dermot with all of me, it's raw and naked and intense.

SELF PORTRAIT
41 CM X 35CM
SCREEN PRINT

15th November, 2001

I feel something in my psyche got disconnected when he died. I'm not sure who I am as if I'm no-one. It feels physical. I've lost a connection to myself. Everything is meaningless. All that afforded a foothold in the past is no longer there, reason, imagination, memory, faith, hope, love, all meaningless. Like a dark night of the soul, a distillation of misery.

I am Rebegot
Of Absence, Darkness and Death,
Things which are not.
JOHN DONNE

20th November, 2001

Tonight is my first night alone in the house since Dermot left. I can't say he died it's just too unreal. We are deeply shocked by death and have much resistance to accepting it even though we know it's inevitable, and we have witnessed it on television innumerable times. Could it mean that somehow we are not meant to die? Death, when our feelings are engaged, becomes an experiential reason for life continuing. I feel that's a comfort. But coming home to an empty house it feels more than an absence; it's like a very scary hole somewhere that makes me feel sick when it creeps up on me.

25th November, 2001

I went to get his death certificate. Seeing his name on it seemed unreal, a mistake. Life going on, people helping me but it seems a game or a drama as if real life will begin again at any moment. I'll be with him telling him what it's been like and he'll be surprised. People say things like "time heals" or "it will become easier" but it doesn't ring true for me. It's hard work to struggle towards a life… a different sort of life. I see it getting worse as I realise more and more that he won't be coming back.

3rd January, 2002

I dream every night about him. The dreams seem like reality because he looks young and well and happy. We hug and I feel close to him. I can even smell him and feel his body. It's life that is like a dream…. a bad one. Love exacts a heavy price.

20th January, 2002

I miss physical contact a lot. I miss his body more than anything, just his physical presence to hug and be held. My body doesn't want to accept that he's gone any more than my heart. I miss his voice and his hands and the way he smelled, his laugh, all of him, his living breathing presence.

1st February, 2002

I made myself go into his workroom today and for the first time I felt maybe it's true he has gone forever. His T-square and his ruler were on his drawing board with his glasses just the way he left them. Ill never be able to sit and watch him drawing again. Never see his lamp lighting and his head bent over the board with that concentrated look on his face when he worked which I loved.

13th February, 2002

I went to a bereavement support group called Bethany. I don't know whether it will help me or not. One of the women there offered to come to the house. I said yes, please do. I need to talk about the confusion of it all and no one I know wants to listen to my repetitions any more.

CONFUSION
71CM X 91CM
OIL & MIXED MEDIA ON CANVAS

DEATH
91CM X 76CM
OIL & MIXED MEDIA ON CANVAS

14th March, 2002

When I'm doing something practical, making a meal for someone coming to visit, or even cleaning, I can manage. I'm in the present. But when I'm alone I begin to remember the past or dread the future. How does one ever recover? I feel homeless even though I have a home. I suppose we were home for each other. I've lost my real home.

24th April, 2002

Six months without Dermot. The passage of time is so relentless. It feels as if I'm moving away, further away from Dermot, further away from my real life. I'm being carried away from October 24th by a machine I can't stop. The year is unfolding; the days getting longer, plants are growing, life continuing. I'm here, part of it, but not part of it. Every thing in me relates back to that time when he died, it's hard even to write that word. But yet I'm being moved on. Everyone says, "hang on, time will heal, one day you'll feel normal." But by that time I won't know normal any more. Normal is having Dermot, talking, laughing, eating, loving, visiting, working, all is meaningless without him. How can I get meaning without him? Where is meaning? I can't imagine a life without him. I tack on to the edges of other peoples' lives. They are the rooted ones, I'm uprooted. When I leave them to come home, emptiness looms up like an iceberg, cold and dark.

28th April, 2002

Listening to *Sunday Miscellany* in the morning, which he loved, makes his absence a deep pain inside me. I can manage to dodge away from the pain when I'm with friends but when I'm alone, which is increasingly more often now, the tide of longing and loneliness rushes back. I think I'll never stop crying. On the outside I seem to be doing well and managing but inside I'm not so sure. The pain is unchanged, worse in fact because everyday it gets more real that he isn't going to come back. Living without him takes so much courage, just to keep trudging along this dark track.

17th May, 2002

We were together so long that we sort of meshed. So when he went, a part of me went too. I'm still not sure who I am. It feels like I'll have to reconstruct myself somehow. But I'm grateful for all I got from him. I could build on the part of him that is now part of me, the things I loved about him.

The way he lived in the present, the way he saw the funny side of things and could make me laugh even when things were dark and his unfailing kindness. I'm clinging to the past and that does not lead to life. He wouldn't like it.

9th September, 2002

Living alone I can do absolutely what I like, but that means I have to desire something I would like to do and find the will to do it. This seems almost impossible but yet I must find some purpose in life. I battle with this all the time. But I have to win this battle to do something. I think maybe I'd like to make a book about Dermot but it is hard to begin. I feel a need to make some sort of statement about his life. I don't want it to disappear unmarked, uncelebrated; all his goodness, and intelligence and uniqueness to not be there anymore. When people die they live only in other peoples' memories and these are processed by the one who remembers. The dead have no voice. I'd like Dermot to be who he was, not just my or other peoples idea of him. I can give him a voice from his diaries. I can write the stories he told me. I'm sure it would help me find out who I am too without him.

20th January, 2003

I'm drawing self-portraits looking in a mirror. It's the first drawing I've done for ages. So far they look as much like my mother or even like Dermot as they do me, a sort of mixture. But it might be another help towards finding myself again.

3rd April, 2003

Looking at the lilac tree waving in the wind this morning I felt a wave of pleasure just as I used to do before life changed. I must be recovering a bit. It's wonderful the way nature is always waiting to be observed and give comfort. It is a real healer when I open myself to its magic and wait for it to enter. I don't always remember.

4th June, 2003

Gordon called today to ask me if I'd put in a question for the discussion group. But I don't feel I want to. I don't seem to have questions or answers anymore. Dermot's death was like a tide that went out washing away all my interest in discussion groups and study groups and theories and talk generally. I'm left washed up on an empty beach holding a shell in my fist. If it contains a pearl it has to be Love. Nothing else means much anymore.

SELF-PORTRAITS
CHARCOAL ON PAPER

RESURRECTION
91CM X 122CM
OIL & MIXED MEDIA ON CANVAS

TOMBPRINT
48cm x 33cm
ETCHING

page 28

5th July, 2003

I've almost finished Dermot's book. I'm feeling very sad. Maybe because the end of it is like reliving two years ago. It looks well enough and the image pages are not too bad but it is a paltry affair really, a collection of facts. What made me think that I could capture something of his soul? All his wit and intelligence and goodness that I will never experience again are now all gone. Sometimes it feels unbearable.

29th November, 2003

I went on the Bethany weekend in Orlagh. It was very helpful but difficult. It opened up the pain again but it was also therapeutic. I spent a lot of the time crying. Two years ago it was like a journey to despair and back. This time I had words for it and I got a lot of support and help to express it and I felt looked after all the time.

be still and wait without hope;
for hope would be hope of the wrong thing;
wait without love,
for love would be love of the wrong thing;...
Wait without thought,
for you are not ready for thought.
T.S. ELIOT

17th February, 2004

Today we would have been 46 years married.

It was a very cold day in 1958 and it snowed later I remember. I felt scared walking up the aisle thinking that maybe I didn't really know him at all. But he looked very serious and concentrated as if he knew what he was doing so then I felt it would be okay. But I didn't realise that morning standing before the altar in University Church on Stephen's Green just how blessed I would be all my life with him.

I went to Olive's Prayer Meeting feeling low. It was a time of prayer and worship where people were free to dance and sing. The hymn tunes reminded me of 1950's dance music. Suddenly I was back in our old house in K.L. The lights low and the doors open to the veranda and the tropical night. When we danced cheek to cheek like one person, just part of the music and making love was like a prayer. God is in dancing and singing but also in my loneliness. I cried but also felt happy. It was such a lovely, unexpectedly strong memory, like an Anniversary present from God.

UNIVERSITY CHURCH, ST. STEPHEN'S GREEN
61CM X 61CM
EMBROIDERY

SELF-PORTRAIT
38cm x 30cm
SCREEN PRINT

DERMOT

Like a boat, I drift rudderless,
Without your steady hand in mine,
My heart still sees you worn by pain,
The tethering tubes no longer lifelines.

At night you come to me in dreams,
With your dark hair falling forward,
Your face intent, over a drawing board,
Strong and tender as when we first loved.

As I drift towards old age
Changed by all your absence brings,
I search a way to live without you
And become someone you may not know.

MARY BRADY, 2002

DUNGANSTOWN

This is your place,
Distilled through summers
To acres of freedom.

If I could pause time
Rewind it, I would find you
There, before our time.

Meet you freewheeling to the sea
Or pedalling back sun-browned,
Tasting of salt.

Join you in the bluebell wood
A young god dancing
Naked through the trees.

Run with you down the darkness
Of the yew walk to the churchyard
And the grass tangled graves.

Run on to where now you wait for me
In one square foot of earth
That holds six feet of you.

MARY BRADY, 2003

DUNGANSTOWN CHURCH
26CM X 38CM
EMBROIDERY ON HANDKERCHIEF

46cm x 44cm
EMBROIDERY ON SHIRT

TIME WITHOUT YOU

I miss your smell
From your jacket I keep
Behind the bedroom door,
Your smell that signalled home to me,
It went quite soon.

Your suits and coat I gave away
They had long grown too big.
But your cap I keep
Uniquely yours, crowning
Your head above the rest, walking
Towards me in the street,
It still holds the shape of you.

I like to think sometimes
That when I hold your drawing pens
The pressure of your hand remains.
And in your chair
Your body imprint holds
A hair, an eyelash hidden.

MARY BRADY, 2003

Walking the Pier

I imagine your fingers woven with mine

in my pocket, walking the pier,

I match your steps, our elbows touch,

We notice birds, a new moon,

the wild smell of seaweed.

Old contentment, warm like a duvet

covers me. Going home

I open the door to silence

dead as blotting paper,

To emptiness heavy like dark air,

To time frozen without you.

Mary Brady, 2005

INTERIOR II
44CM X 33CM
EMBROIDERY

TO DERMOT

Now I have friends you will never meet,

I have seen places you will never visit

I have learned things I can never tell you.

But without your certainty I have only questions

Without your warmth winter remains longer.

Without your love I no longer belong.

With your absence loneliness fills your place.

MARY BRADY, SEPTEMBER 2005

POSTSCRIPT

This book is a record of my Journey through Grief, and the many ways I tried to deal with the pain and make sense of the loss of my husband. I offer it in the hope that it will be a help and encouragement to others who are struggling through the bewildering pain and misery of bereavement.

It is now eight years since my husband's death. I have survived, though there were days when I wasn't sure I would. His loss will always be a presence in my life though it no longer fills my every waking moment. His love will always be an encouragement and an inspiration for me.

My search for meaning has led me down new paths and in ways I haven't expected. I have met many people on the same journey and have been blessed by them.

Bethany has remained an important part of my life. I am grateful for the help and support it has given me.

Mary Brady, October 2009

Les Amis du Chemin de Sa.
Pyrénées-Atlantiques

délivré par :

39, rue de la Citadelle
F-64220 SAINT-JEAN-PIED-DE-PORT
Tél. 05 59 37 05 09
aucoeurduchemin.org

N° 7620

Pour obtenir à Saint-Jacques de Compostelle "LA
COMPOSTELLA", faites tamponner à chaque étape.

DATE ET CACHET DE LA HALTE
FIRMAS Y SELLOS

Posada de Roncesvalles
Teléfono 948 760225
31850 RONCESVALLES
(Navarra)

CARNET DE PÈLERIN
DE SAINT-JACQUES
"Credencial del Peregrino"

IGLESIA CATEDRAL
BURGOS
16-9-04

SANTA MARIA DE MIRAFLORES
BURGOS
16/IX/04

Camino de Santiago
17 SEP 2004
«Fontanas»

ESTELLA

Santo Domingo
de la Calzada
La Rioja

DERMOT'S BOOK

...btenir à Saint-Jacques de Compostelle "LA
"STELLA", faites tamponner à chaque étape.
...TE ET CACHET DE LA HALTE
FIRMAS Y SELLOS

Posada de Roncesvalles
Teléfono 948 76022...
31650 RO...

DATE ET CACHET DE LA HALTE
FIRMAS Y SELLOS

IGLESIA CATEDRAL

EL ACEBO

BLESSED ARE THOSE WHOSE
STRENGTH IS IN YOU,
WHO HAVE SET THEIR HEART
ON PILGRIMAGE.
AS THEY PASS THROUGH THE
VALLEY OF DESOLTION
THEY MAKE IT A PLACE OF SPRINGS.

PSALM 84